First World War
and Army of Occupation
War Diary
France, Belgium and Germany

28 DIVISION
84 Infantry Brigade
Welsh Regiment
1st Battalion
5 July 1915 - 31 July 1915

WO95/2277/4

The Naval & Military Press Ltd
www.nmarchive.com
Published in association with The National Archives

Published by

The Naval & Military Press Ltd

Unit 10 Ridgewood Industrial Park,

Uckfield, East Sussex,

TN22 5QE England

Tel: +44 (0) 1825 749494

www.naval-military-press.com

www.nmarchive.com

This diary has been reprinted in facsimile from the original. Any imperfections are inevitably reproduced and the quality may fall short of modern type and cartographic standards.

© **Crown Copyright**
Images reproduced by permission of The National Archives, London, England, 2015.

Contents

Document type	Place/Title	Date From	Date To
Heading	1/6th Battalion The Welsh Regiment July 1915-October 1915		
Heading	28th Division 84th Infy Bde 6th Bn Welsh Regt Jly-Oct 1915 To 1 Din 3 Bde		
Heading	84th Inf. Bde. 28th Div. Battn. posted to Bde. 5.7.15 from L. of C. 1/6th Battn. The Welsh Regiment. July (5/31.7.15) 1915		
War Diary		05/07/1915	31/07/1915
Heading	84th Inf. Bde. 28th Div. 1/6th Battn. The Welsh Regiment. August 1915		
Miscellaneous	Battn Bathing. 2nd Aug	01/08/1915	01/08/1915
Heading	84th Inf. Bde. 28th Div. 1/6th Battn. The Welsh Regiment. September 1915		
Miscellaneous			
Heading	84th Inf. Bde. 28th Div. Battn. transferred to 3rd Inf. Bde. 1st Div. 23.10.15. 1/6th Battn. The Welsh Regiment. October 1915		
Miscellaneous			

28TH DIVISION
84TH INFY BDE

6TH BN WELSH REGT
JLY - OCT 1915

To 1 DIV 3 BDE

84th Inf.Bde.
28th Div.

Battn. posted to
Bde. 5.7.15 from
L. of C.

1/6th BATTN. THE WELSH REGIMENT.

J U L Y

(5/31.7.15)

1915

War Diary

of the 1/6 Batt The Welsh Regiment

For the Period 5th July to 31st July 1915 (Inclusive)

1915

July 5th — Left WISERNES by Busses for LA CLYTTE. 84th Brigade, 28th Division, 2nd Corps 2nd Army. Strength 20 Officers 934 Other Ranks.
Lt Col Lord N.E. Crichton Stuart.
Major E.M.S Morgan (Senior Major)   Major L. Thomas (Quarter Master)
Capt Carleton. Adjutant.   Capt Browning   Capt Gibbon
Capt Golaberg.   Lt. Harris.   Lt Lewis.   Lt Hawkins.   Lt Langer
2/Lt Brown M. Gun.   2/Lt Frisby,   2/Lt Roberts,   2/Lt Webb,   2/Lt Shuttlewood
2/Lt Evans.   2/Lt Davies.   2/Lt Williams   Sneath R.A.M.C.

Arrived LA CLYTTE 10 A.M. and met by Brigadier General Boles, 6md Brigade
Bivouaced in Tents and Shelters

July 6th — Inspected by General Boles.
Lt Lewis to Command of C. Coy vice Cann to England.
Lt Davies to Transport vice Lewis
Col Crichton Stuart and Capt Carleton went round Battalion Head Quarters with Brigadier
Trenches really Breastworks of Sand Bags
A + C Coys to Trenches for 24 Hours and B and D Coys Digging

July 7th — Digging Parties return. No Casualties.

July 8th — Colonel and Adjutant to Head Quarters of 1st Welsh for night

July 9th — Colonel and Adjutant went round Trenches of 1st Welsh with Major Toke
Digging Parties work at night

July 10th — Digging Parties return. One Man of D Coy hit (not serious)

July 11th — Digging Parties work at night

July 12th — Capt Pritchard, Capt Shaw, and Capt Jeffreys arrived

July 13th — Lts Bell, Price, Clarry, and Lindsay Brabazon Arrived
Digging Parties work at night

July 14th — Order to move to WESTOUTRE

July 15th — Marched out 8.15 P.M. via RENINGHELST to WESTOUTRE.
Head Qrs of Batt: at VERDOONCK Farm. C. Coy in a Farm,
D Coy in another, A + B Coys together.

July 16th   A Coy under Capt Browning go into Trenches of
             1st Welsh Regt
             C. Coy under Capt Pritchard go into Trenches of 2nd Cheshire Regt

"   17th   March to LOCRE Starting 10 A.M. Billeted at LOCREHOF Farm
             and in Fire Huts.

"   18th   Colonel and Adjutant round Trenches of 2 Cheshires,
             and 1 Welsh Regts to see Companies of the Battalion.

"   19th   Major Morgan and Adjutant round Trenches
             A Coy come out of Trenches with 1st Welsh Regt
             B Coy under Capt Gibbon to Trenches with Monmouth Regt
             in relief of 1st Welsh Regt

"   20th   Lft Evans Posted to Reserve Battery R.F.A. and struck off Strength
             Authorities A.G. No 4/5713 of 17/7/15
             C. Coy returned from Trenches with 2/Cheshire Regt
             D Coy under Capt Pritchard, and one Machine Gun under
             Sgt Thatcher to Trenches with 1 Suffolk Regt in relief
             of 2 Cheshire Regt   2274 Pte Shoemake.(C Coy)(M.G) Killed
             with C. Coy on 16th July one Machine Gun under
             Lft Browne to Trenches and returned on 20th July.

"   21st   1066 Cpl J Davies B. Coy Killed
             Lft Williams. W.S. Wounded Foot & Leg
             Major Morgan round Trenches
             Officers (3) reconnoitred VERSTRAAT. SWITCH
             and G. H.Q 2nd Line Trenches.

"   22nd   Three Officers reconnoitred G. H.Q 2nd Line

"   23rd   Garrisons sent to S.P. 8, 9, 10, 11
             Officers of Garrisons Capt Goldberg, Lt Lewis, Lt Wells
             and Lt Shuttlewood
             Battalion moved LOCRE to ARCADIA Dug-outs at KEMMEL

July 24th — Men on Fatigue making Dug-outs Etc
1742 Pte W. G. Butcher B Coy Killed

" 25th — B & D Coys relieved from Trenches and arrive KEMMEL Dug-outs
B was Attached 1st Welsh Regt. and D to Suffolks

" 26th — S.P. 8, 9, 10, 11, Trenches visited by Colonel and Adjutant

" 27th — S.P. 10 & 11 relieved (Lt. Lewes and Lt. Wells.)
SP 8 & 9 visited. Work on Dug-outs at KEMMEL

" 28th — S P 8 & 9 relieved (Capt. Goldberg and Lt. Shuttlewood)

" 29th — 2085 Pte. S. Lewis D Coy wounded in Ankle

" 30th — 1951 Pte Welsh wounded in Jaw carrying for
Cheshires (in Communication Trench)
200 Carrying, 230 Digging on VIERSTRAAT Etc.

" 31st — 40 Shells fired at ARCADIA Dug-outs
Lt. Mills, 1992 Pte. Howells. B. 1872 Pte Clarke
2350 Pte Furze. G. Wounded.
Relieved by Suffolk Regt. and left for LOCRE to bath
60 Men under Lt Harries remained for Mining.
—————— 11 ——————

84th Inf.Bde.
28th Div.

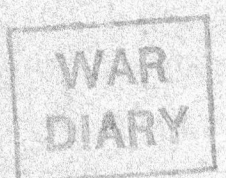

1/6th BATTN. THE WELSH REGIMENT.

A U G U S T

1 9 1 5

1/6th Battalion The Welsh Regiment.

August 1915

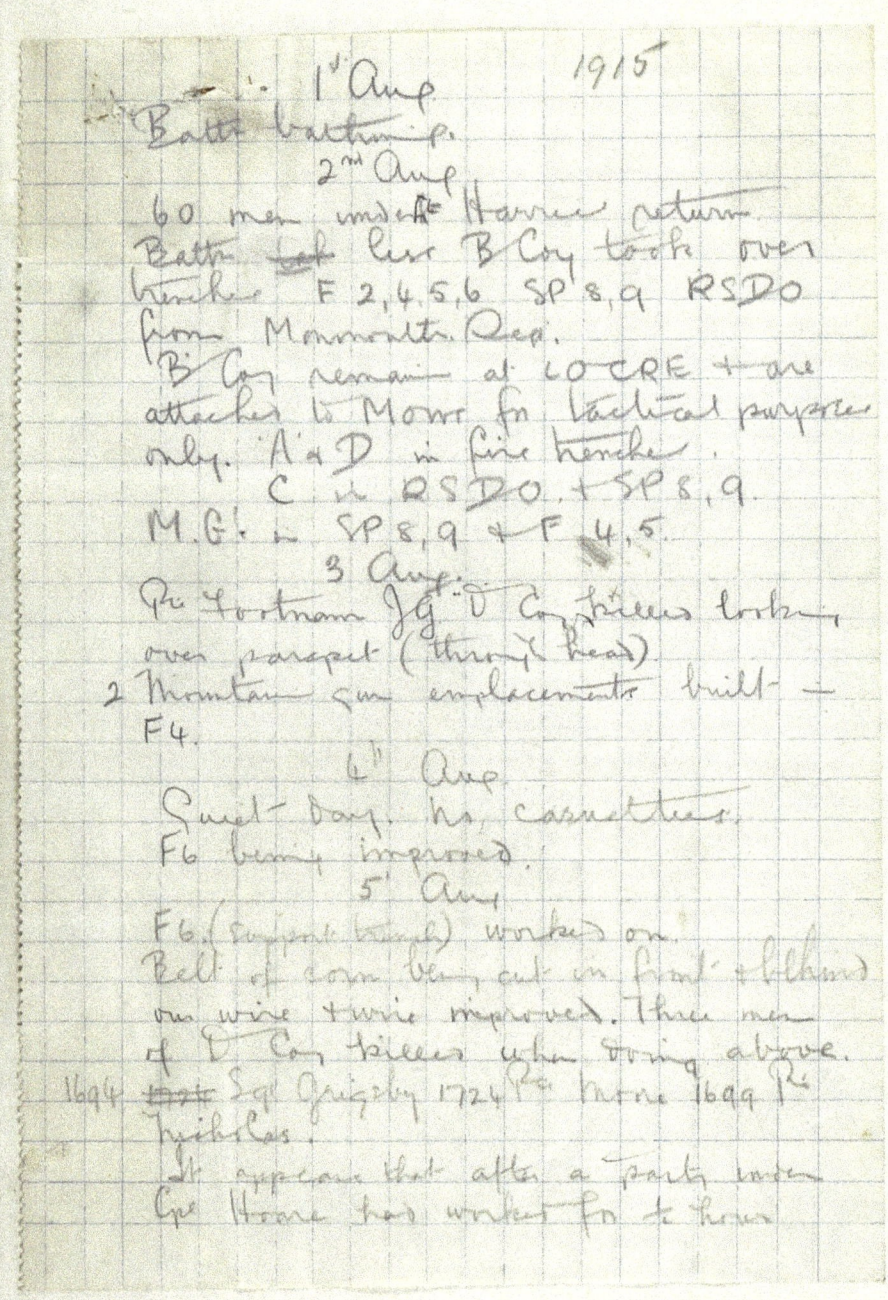

5 Aug (cont.)

Pte Moore was hit in knee. Cpl Hoare then moved the party back & stayed behind himself to bandage. He next saw Pte Nicholas, a great friend of Moore, coming towards them, evidently to help. Just before reaching them Nicholas dropped. Cpl Hoare then left Moore for Nicholas & found him dead. Moore was soon after hit in the head whilst being dressed by Cpl Hoare who had again come back to him. After the Cpl had reported the affair to Capt Pritchard it was decided to go out towards the two men. During the scuppering Sgt Quigley rose out in front & was immediately hit. The three men, all dead, were recovered after dark.

2296 Pte Jones died from abdominal injury after accident in transport lines.

C. Coys, belonging to 83 Bde on our right asked what the Reg' is as there L with the coloured ribbon on their Shoulder (armlets). C. Coys answer "The Canadian Sharpshooters".

6 Aug.
Quiet day. Enemy observed working opposite D Coy. Arty turned on & hit our part of parapet

6 Aug (cont)

1 N.C.O. + 12 men (trenchmen) sent to Mining Section from 'B' Coy. There are now 50 men employed with mining section. Lt Davies R.T.O on leave. Lt Lewis temporary R.T.O.

7 Aug

8 whizzbangs fell between SP 9 & RSDO a 4.7 shell (very erratic flight) fell near RSDO, shell recovered but unable to trace battery which fired it.
Very quiet day. B Coy (all MONS) move from KEMMEL shelters to LOCRE.
Lt Lindsay Brabazon & Cpt Murphrid to MG school at WISQUES for course.

8 Aug

To prepare for possible retaliation for a Artillery shoot arranged for 9 Aug narrow trenches made behind fire trenches. Arranged for garrison of Regent Street dug outs to take cover on MUMBLES ROAD.

9 Aug

Arty shoots 4ᵃᵐ till 4.10 & 4.20 till 4.60
H.Q. moved to Batt Battle HQ at REGENT STREET Dugouts during shoot. Shoot to support attack on trenches at HOOGE. These were taken

10 Aug.
Battalion less B Coy & one MG relieved. F2 + supports & F2 & SP 8, 9 by SUFFOLKS. F 3, 4 + supports by N ~~NORTH~~ NORTH. FUS.
B Coy take over REGENT STREET dug outs.
Relief completed 4 a.m. Late from owing to SUFFOLK relieving party losing its way.
Battalion moved to billets at LOCRE.

11 Aug.
Company drill etc.

12 Aug.
989 L/c Edwards wounded in chest. B Coy.
130 dig on VIERSTRAAT line
100 carry for MINING section.

13 Aug.
N Brown sent to BAILLEUL sick.
Company drill. New VICKERS light gun issued.

14 Aug.
Bathing at LOCRE. Refitting with boots.

15 Aug.
Took over trenches from 7/LEICESTERS. NORTH FUS. 2/CHESHIRE. Relief completed 11.35 p.

16 Aug.
C.O. went round trenches with new Brigade Major. MG belt issued with new pattern

tube smoke-helmet. Lt Roberts
returned from leave. Lt Shuttleworth
left for leave.

17 Aug.
F5, 6 + supports in F6 handed over
to 1 WELCH. A & B Coys to LOCRE
B+ issued with telescopic sighted
rifle.

18 Aug
E3 handed over to 1 SUFFOLK REGT
Much water in trenches & communication
trenches + many falls caused by
the rain.
Major Morgan to LOCRE
Lt WELLS took over MGuns from
Lt Brown 14th Aug

19 Aug
Lt Wells in trenches building MG
emplacement in F2.
II Corps Commander Gen'l Ferguson
visited trenches of Brigade. Not
very pleased & report of trenches
held by 84 B+ not good.
Gen'l Bols, Maj Gepp (Bde Maj) &
Cap+ Monkswell (Bde MG Off) dined

at Church 19 Aug

20 Aug
Conference of C.O's at B'n H.Q.
to receive points noted by II Corps
Cmdt & also about winter quarters.

POINTS NOTED during inspection
of Brigade trenches by II Corps Cmdt.

I Some respirators hung up on
  trenches.
II Quantity of SAA lying about
III Rifles to be kept in racks
IV No notice boards erected for R.A telephones
V No unpierced cards be found. These
  must be collected & broken ones returned
  to workshop. Any broken grenade
  tins are to be returned
VI Rifles & SAA both in the magazine &
  that carried on the men are to be
  inspected daily
VII All telephone wires not in use to
  be removed. All wires must run
  along a trench & be properly fastened
VIII Several sprayers were seen but nobody
  knew where the anti gas solution
  was kept. These are to be kept together
  & the place known to the men who are
  detailed to use them

IX. The wiring of our trenches throughout is bad, also the parapet throughout requires repairing with sandbags. These two things are to be taken in hand at once & progress made reported each day in daily report. The repairing of the parapet can be done by day by the men on wire business.

X. In many places the parapet has been heightened so that the firing step is too low for the men to fire over the parapet. This must be rectified.

XI. There is still a great deal of filth empty tins etc in rear of some of the trenches.

The GOC wishes that terrible attention be by the Brigade Offr comdg were used orders that Equipment are to be regularly and takes all trench stores which he out of repair collected & returns to Base ROC.

24 July.

... in front of
F6 ... two ... under heavy
... appearing to ... quiet well.
Two MGs ... shells fell on
Kimberley, one in F3 one in F6 there
were no ... at F6.

25 July.

Rather heavy ... Bombing of
line continued ... was on
Kimberley.
Communication trench from F2 to F6
is running in front of F6 by men sent
from other Coy to the Brigade.

26 Aug.

Colonel O.C. left for leave. Major Morgan
took over command.
Great news from the BALTIC. One super
Dreadnought, 2 cruisers, 7 destroyers &
a boat ... landing party sunk near
RIGA.
Enemy put up a hurdle in front of E2
within our lines. 2356 Pte Davies K Coy
who himself was ... of this war
killed.
12 men ... from ROUEN (hospital)
Non coal boxes fell between X roads & CHAPET

24 Aug. 20 men from No 8 C Coy at LOCRE reported at 9ᵃᵐ for work in PALL MALL. This party is being detailed daily till finished above. A "Coalbox" fell on edge of PALL MALL about 10 yds from this party & filled in the trench. This was cleared away.
Permanent fatigue in VIGO STREET has done good work, but party in REGENT STREET not so good. A corpl with knowledge of draining is wanted & C Coy has been asked to supply one. Not inspected work as after rain, little rains the panel traverse in many places are awash. Drains must now be made under centre of trench boards & not at sides as it is found that with drain at side the trench boards soon become undermined & consequently fall in.

25 Aug. Party of 20 with L Bull reported at 9ᵃᵐ for work on PALL MALL.
SUFFOLKS in EI sang & called to the Germans all the night of the 23-24 (night of move of BALTIC hop) much to their annoyance. Divl memorandy today forbids any conversation with enemy or exchange of newspapers.

25. (pm) - Genl Bols on leave. Col tinch Pearse CHESHIRE to temporary command.
Adjt Reporters visited trenches.
All spare wire cleared from communication trenches for trenches.
Position for shell trenches to be made in trenches. First F.6, F.2.

26 Aug. Proposed reliefs from 24 Aug to 20 Sept.
6th & 7th WELCH alternately remaining in LOCRE.

	Aug										Sept																				
---	24	25	26	27	28	29	30	31	1	2	3	4	5	6	7	8	9	10	11	12	13	14	15	16	17	18	19	20
6 WELCH	L	L	L	L	R	L	L	L	L	L	R	L	L	L	L	L	R	L	L	L	L	L	R	L	L	L	L	L

R. Night relieved.
L Night at LOCRE + used for fatigues
L Nights at LOCRE + not used for fatigues.

Aircraft passed over F.2 travelling from SE direction at 10.30pm. No lights & it was not seen. It is believed to have circled round me before going away. Officer reporting this L' Clarry.
Capt Gibbon, O.C. E.2 reports that he believes a British converted M.G. is firing from a redoubt + enemy lines in front of SPANBROEK MOLEN.
However the relative position of SP. 5, 9 held by middle belt of thunderer in between and L WELCH

27 Aug. Garrison of F₁ & F₂ strength
D. 6 O.R.'s (Knatake 2 mm)
Considerable time is being spent on
clearing up the trenches, about 40
bags of "Empty Cases" have
been collected from E₂ & F₂.
The re-facing of the parapet is still
in progress, & good work is being
done.
The wiring in front of F6 done by
this Battn. was complimented on
by the Brigade Major.

28 Aug. Snipers observing from E₂ report
enemy's posts were found, but no
rounds fired owing to lack of
movement. O.C. Snipers condemns
existing loopholes & proposes the following.
1. Pall Mall communication trench, point
 on left 100 yds from end.
2. House in rear of F6 Trench
3. Rise on left of F6 Trench in front of
 STORE Farm on Contour 74.
4. Angle of E₂ Trench.
The above positions will be used
alternately.
A series of Dummy Sniping Posts
are under construction.
        Maintenance & improvement has
been carried out in all trenches.

27 Aug (con'd)
C & D Companies relieved A & B in Trenches E2 E6, & F2 & F6. A & B Companies proceeded to Swansea Shelters.

29th Aug. While digging communication trench between F2 & F3, machine gun fire was directed on them, which prevented further work by day. The work was resumed by night & the two trenches connected up, further improvements of above are in hand. Wiring in front of F6 is still in progress.

Permanent fatigue in communication Trench report considerable progress. Supports 8 & 9 have dug shell Trenches & completed drainage.

Snipers observe that Uniform worn by enemy opposite us is Dark blue, & not grey blue as previously seen, the caps are the same.

30th Aug. General repair and improvement was carried out in the fire trenches. Patrols were sent out, but had nothing to report.
Wiring & drainage was the chief

30th Aug (contd)

feature in yesterdays support
posts work. Good work was
done in front of F.6. by working
party, which should be
completed today.
Shell trenches & strengthening
of dugouts was also continued.
Lieut Mills returned from Hospital
& rejoined C Company in the
trenches.
Lieut Wells. M.G. Officer was
warmly thanked by Brigade
Major, for the most excellent
map of district & trenches
compiled him.
The Snipers report considerable
activity around the enemy's
line, several digging parties
being fired on by above &
two enemy hit

31st August

Both the permanent and
extra fatigues working on the
communication trenches did
good work in draining &
relaying trench boards
The supports have been busy

31st Aug (contd)
digging shell shelters and
revetting communication trench.
Knife rests and trip wire were
put out in front of E2.
Re facing & rebuilding dugouts
was also done in the fire trenches
The communication trench leading
from F2 – F6 still requires
a little deepening & widening
otherwise it is complete.
Fifty yards of wiring is all
that is needed to complete
wiring in front of F.6.
Our Patrol reported Enemy's
wire good in places.
Captain Pritchard of D. Coy
went to Hospital with Influenza

84th Inf.Bde.
28th Div.

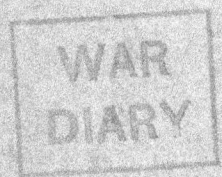

1/6th BATTN. THE WELSH REGIMENT.

S E P T E M B E R

1 9 1 5

1/6th Battalion The Welsh Regiment.

September 1915

September 1st

The work of drainage and building dugouts, & refacing is still in progress on the fire trenches.

F.6 has made good progress on the communication trench but was delayed considerably by machine gun fire & the fire from a fixed rifle.

A formidable obstacle of wire is now nearing completion from Pall Mall to Piccadilly.

The snipers report renewed activity both behind & in front of the German lines. General Bulfin G.O.C. Division visited our lines, & expressed himself well with the general appearance of both trenches & men.

Lt. R. SHUTTLEWOOD was wounded the afternoon in the arm and leg by a shell, while walking down communication trench PALL MALL.

Sept. 2nd Today we have been the recipients of a good many enemy

Sept 2nd (Cont'd)

souvenirs, who alternately shelled the supports & battery, & no shells fell all around us, but none actually hit the building.

The Parados at S.P.5 was knocked down & one man of the Monmouths was killed.

Very little work was done on the Fire trenches owing to the continual downpour of rain.

The drainage system received immediate attention, & was materially improved.

In all, about 300 ft of the Comm Trench PALL MALL was drained & sides revetted, & where necessary boards renewed, & replaced.

Our snipers report that enemy are particularly busy in front of F.2. wiring all around the ruined house, & digging new sap between two fronts. An Engine can distinctly be heard & occasionly steam has been seen. Patrols searched neighbouring farms for suspicious persons but had nothing to report.

Sept 3rd A & B companies relieved

Sept 3rd (cont'd)

C & D. Companies in the trenches. It has been wet all day & very stormy during the night, so very little work apart from drainage has been carried out. The snipers report that a steam trench digger is at work just south of the BLACK REDOUBT. This will in all probability receive our attention very shortly.

To-day is noteworthy for the conspicuous absence of shells.

Sept 4th Owing to the heavy rains, the majority of the work has been draining & rebuilding collapsed dugouts, & revetting & general repair.

We shelled the BLACK REDOUBT & a place behind SPANBROEK MOLEN where the Steam Engine was with heavy Artillery, & with good effect. The snipers report the Engine has not been working since.

Carrier pigeons were observed going over towards the enemy's lines last night & coming

Sept 4 (cont'd)

the direction of KENNEL. They were not our Pigeons & have not returned.

Lieut BURNIE reported here for duty & proceeded to R.S.D.O.

Sept 5th

Draining trenches, clipping sumps & re-setting trench Boards & general imperative repairs to the parapet were carried out to-day. Owing to the sodden nature of the ground, several places have given away in the supports which requires immediate attention. Some wiring was also done.

Considerable drainage & revetting has been done in the Communication Trenches VIGO St & REGENT St.

Sept 6th

The work of refacing the parapet & re-building dug-outs is in progress.

Shell Trenches are being dug in all the Communication Trenches.

The Snipers report that after careful observation of the house about 100 yds N.W. of

Sept 6. (Cont'd)

E1, the house nearest our line is used for burning rubbish but both are fortified and a machine gun emplacement in front of E6? infiledeling flank of E1. The nearest house is also used as a listening post.
We bagged one German yesterday.

Sept 7. Good work has been done in the repairing of the parapet, a lot remains to be done, but the back of the job is broken.
The enemy last night removed what is commonly called the DUMMY GUN in front of F.2. This object is really one of the arms of SPANBROEKE MOULEN, & has proved a good landmark for our artillery.
The Snipers put the artillery on to a working party of the enemy this morning, which effectually stopped progress in that direction.

Sept 8th Evidently the enemy have a good supply of Steam Engines because another one was reported working on the same

Sept 8th (con'd)
place this morning.
They are apparently making
SPANBROUKE MOLEN into a REDOUBT.
Very little is actually happening
but there seems just that stir
in the air that heralds big
things.

Sept 9th Today we shelled the
BLACK REDOUBT with High
explosives, with good outward
results, a good deal of their
parapet was knocked down,
and judging from the amount
of earth etc that has been
thrown up from there, some
mess was made inside.
C & D. Coys relieved A & B. Coys
in the trenches. The whole
relief was completed by 9.30 pm
this is the record to date.
Lt FRISBY came back from leave
& Lt LANGER went on leave.
The work in the trenches at the
present time chiefly consists
of re-facing the parapet &
slipping shell trenches, & repairing
the firing platform, some
wiring was also done

Sept 9th (cont'd)
A Patrol of ours last night reported that they could hear the enemy driving stakes & timber in houses West of E1, in the gully where fire is always seen. No working party was visible.

Sept 10th Shell trenches are being dug with great activity, also general repairs are everywhere being executed.
Troops were seen passing through WYCHEATE just at dusk. Their progress was estimated & they were shelled.
The enemy continue to fortify SPANBROUKE MOULEN, and be repairing the whole of the front line trenches generally.

Sept 11th The permanent men on the communication trenches are doing good work, & having finished PALL MALL are now busy with REGENT ST, in which they have dug a drain & relayed boards for a distance of about 100 yds. The same work in the fire trenches continues today as yesterday. A Patrol

Sept 11th (contd)

examined the enemy's wire yesterday which they reported as good with no gaps. Some fresh wire has been placed near their extended sap in front of F.2.

Sept 12th

We shelled the BLACK REDOUBT again today both with heavy & light explosive shells and fairly knocked the place about. The enemy retaliated with whiz-bangs, one of which set the old farm & Hayrick on fire behind S.P.5, a machine gun & rifle fire was directed on the conflagration, which prevented communication to S.P.5 so another trench was started skirting the Farm.

A working party were observed placing wire round their extended sap in front of F.2, a little rapid fire from the garrison of 5 bays assisted by a machine gun traversing over the parapet was used & the work was not further proceeded with during the night

Sept 12th cont'd)
A mountain Gun and some Trench Mortars poured explosives into the ruined houses in front of E.2., owing to one very large explosion, it is thought that an ammunition store was hit. These houses are now razed to the ground.
Our snipers observed an enemy M.G. emplacement about 100 yds. N.W. of SPANBROUKE MOULEN.
Working party seen, & steam pump working, discharging water & steam, this morning, alongside the houses we shelled the night before.
Lt FRISBY took over the Transport & Lt DAVIES went into the trenches

Sept 14th The work of repairing the parapet, & completing the shell trenches is still in progress. In E7 nearly five new dugouts are completed. A party working on the C.T. to S.P.8 have lowered the line at an average depth of three feet.
An Enemy working party seen

Sept 13th Nothing to report.

Sept 14th (cont'd)

40 yds left N.W. of SPANBROUKE MOULEN large pieces of timber being laid in the trench. The Artillery were informed, & operations stopped. Heavy Artillery put 7 shells right on to BLACK REDOUBT. Enemy making small saps just in front of SPANBROUKE MOULEN, it is thought they intend to join up to extended sap in front of F.2.

Sept 15th

The work of drainage and refacing is continuing & satisfactory progress is being made.

Enemy have been seen carrying stakes & timber that looks like match boarding to a point in their trench about 40 yds N.W. of SPANBROEKE MOULEN. Our Artillery dispersed them. The fire in empty house in front of F2 is surmised to be merely a blind to hide the pump working in the sap below it. A trench mortar played on these houses with good effect.

Sept 16th

All energy is now being expended on the clipping of shell trenches, which are now nearing completion.

The Huns put some shells on our Guard & Dumping ground, but no damage was done.

Enemy very quiet, even the snipers report no activity behind the lines.

We were to have shelled the BLACK REDOUBT today but owing to mist it was postponed.

Sept 17th

Considerable progress has been made in the refacing of the parapet which is now nearing completion.

The BLACK REDOUBT has 17 large shells (9.2) placed on it. SPANBROUKE MOULEN also had 3 large shells placed into it. The enemy replied with 17 coal boxes, which did not do any damage.

Sept 18th

Refacing the parapet drainage & building dugouts

Sept 18th Cont'd
has been the chief feature of
todays work.
The enemy was very busy
shelling all along our line
for about 4 hours in
retaliation for the doing
we gave them yesterday.
Two Bays in F2 were
blown down but no one
was injured. Inspite the
heavy shelling no other
damage was done.
One of our Biplanes was
brought down seemingly
by Rifle fire, it volplaned
into safety.
Enemy working party
observed mending their
parapet, & was observed
dispersed by our Artillery.
Sept 19th During the day all
hands were busy refacing
the parapet & building
dugouts, & draining.
The Huns who continued
yesterday, & they persistently
shelled our trenches
with coal boxes. Bays

Sept 19 to 16th [?]

17 & 18 were blown in, but no one was hurt, these Bays were repaired during the night. One shell fell in PALL MALL between F4 & F2 this was also cleared. Cold East wind but brilliant sunshine.

Sept 20th

We were relieved today by the 13th Canadian Highlanders, a very flash one were too, it has been quite all day, we surmise the Hun having got rid of all surplus Ammunition the last two days.

A & B Companies & Headquarters moved back to LOCRE & joined C & D Companies, the whole of the 74th Brigade is billited around LOCRE.

Sept 21st

We all marched off at 9.30 am scenes of great activity, the whole Brigade moving. We marched past the Lt. Gen. Sir Charles FERGUSON General BULFIN in BAILLEUL, who has since expressed him self & approval

Sept 21st (contd)

of their appearance.
It was very hot indeed & men were falling out all along the route. Allowance must be made, as the men had not taken off their boots for over a week. We arrived at PRADELLES about 3.0 p.m. & proceeded to make ourselves comfortable.

Sept 22nd

The whole of the morning was spent in cleaning Rifles & Ammunition, & foot inspection. Latrines were dug as well as grease pits & trench tables. A short route march was indulged in during the afternoon.

Sept 23rd

A route march of about 10 miles was carried out this morning. About 40 men fell out, those who were examined & passed as medically fit were severely dealt with. In the afternoon the Companys paraded independently & were practised in expect fire, motions only, & Platoon drill.

Sept 24th

General B. Finch Pearse, the Brigadier of our Brigade inspected us this morning, some slight difference of opinion about the men's ammunition and equipment led to a fresh lot being indented for.
In spite of the rain the men went a route march for about 6 miles, no men fell out.

Sept 26th

To-day was set apart for rest we started early by parading at 9 o'clock a.m. ready to march out. We started off & went through MERVILLE & eventually billeted in PARADIS

Sept 29th

At 7 o'clock this morning we had orders to parade & embuss at 9.30 am. This was successfully carried the whole Brigade embussing. We stopped at BETHUNE, & from there marched through BEUVRY & LA BOURSE to SAILLY LA BOURSE. We took up our Billets in the latter place

Sept 28th Cont'd.

A & D Companys in Baras & C & B Companys advancing. It is very cold with intermittent showers. Great scenes of activity & excitement are taking place. Muddy & wounded soldiers coming in, while line after line of Transport & Ambulances going up to the line.

Sept 29th

Today we are the Reserve Battalion ready to move out at half an hours notice. All is prepared & the men are very keen to get up to the Line. The 9th Camerons came in today looking very much the worse for wear and shellshocked but cheerful. The weather is still unfavourable.

Sept 30th

At 3:30 p.m. today we were suddenly called up & marched out of SAILLY LA BOURSE by 4:0 p.m. After a short but tedious march we arrived at ANNEQUIN, where after standing several hours in the rain & cold awaiting orders, we sought

Sept 29th (contd)

a letter to some of the
recent losses of this once
pretty little mining village.

Sept 30th

Special attention was paid to
Bombing practice this morning.
Inspection of Rifles and
ammunition also took place.
At 5.0 p.m. we were ordered to
parade at 5.30 ready to go
to the trenches. The whole
Brigade was moved up &
away we went arriving at
VERMELLES about 9 p.m. where
we drew Bombs, Ammunition
tools etc. Just one moved on
to BARTS DUMP where we
waited the major for time of
the night in the Wet & cold,
finally taking over our
trenches at 9.30 am on Oct 1st
very cold & miserable.

84th Inf.Bde.
28th Div.

Battn. transferred
to 3rd Inf.Bde. 1st
Div. 23.10.15.

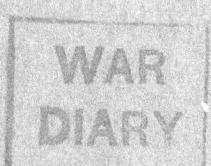

1/6th BATTN. THE WELSH REGIMENT.

O C T O B E R

1 9 1 5

1/6th Battalion The Welsh Regiment.

October 1915

October 1st 1915.

These Trenches come as a bit of a shock to us, who have always been used to perfectly cleaned & drained ones. But fighting is the order of the day & everything else goes by the board.

In front of us is a Redoubt called HOHENZOLLERN Redoubt, to the North of which runs a trench called LITTLE WILLIE & to the South BIG WILLIE. The English held part of the Redoubt & all of BIG WILLIE. At 7.0 pm we had orders to attack & capture LITTLE WILLIE, this was cancelled & the 1st Welsh made the attack at 7.0 pm, this was successful we reinforced them & also supplied them with Bombs and Ammunition. Lt. BRABAZON returned from the right of LITTLE WILLIE with with part of his Company as he had orders that LITTLE WILLIE was getting too crowded. Many casualties occurred in transferring Bombs etc across to LITTLE WILLIE, but the work was carried on throughout the night.

Lt. HAWKINS was shot through the neck whilst leading his Company, the attack, & he seemed sure he had to fall.

Oct 2nd

At 3.0 am today the O.C. 6th Welsh visited LITTLE WILLIE and decided that a Communication Trench must be dug to part of LITTLE WILLIE held by the 1st and 6th Welsh from the NEW TRENCH. This was started immediately from both ends but owing to difficulties the work was delayed.

During the day up to 3.30 pm continual work was carried out on the New Sap, while continual Bombing was taking place in LITTLE WILLIE.

At 3.30 pm LITTLE WILLIE was evacuated by the 1st & 6th Welsh owing to the Bombing by the enemy & the exhaustion of Bombs with which to reply.

Immediately after this, the East end of the NEW TRENCH was vigorously Bombed by the enemy. The Bomb stores here were successfully removed. While superintending this and encouraging the men, our Colonel LORD NINIAN-CRICHTON-STUART

2nd Lt. BURNE was killed by this afternoon this morning

Oct. 2nd (Cont'd)
was mortally shot through the head, death being instantaneous. His Body was placed in a Zinc & wood coffin & conveyed to BETHUNE, where he was placed in the CAVE in the Public Cemetry on Oct 4th 1915.
At 12 o'clock midnight the 2nd Cheshires & 1st Suffolks attempted to retake LITTLE WILLIE, for this purpose the 6th Welsh retired into the Support Trenches, again manning the Fire Trench immediately after the attack.
The garrison of ~~LITTLE WILLIE~~ NEW TRENCH supplemented by Bombers of 1st Welsh, Suffolks & Cheshires bombed L.W. immediately in front of end of Sap & were ordered to take Bombs over at all costs. The attack having failed a barricade was put up 7 yds from East end of NEW TRENCH and Bombers organised to resist attack. Intermittent Bombing & Trench Mortar bombs for the rest of day

October 3rd
Today has been spent in reorganising the Battalion which had become mixed up with various other Regiments. Arrangements were also made for our relief and at 5.30 pm the K.O.Y.L.I. relieved the Battalion.
We marched back to ANNEQUIN & on arriving at Billets were sent back to the support lines LANCASTER LINE near VERMELLES. We also supplied a fatigue party of 400 men.

October 4th
We are still in support ready to move away at a moments notice. Deficiencies in Ammunition Smoke Helmets & Iron Rations are being made up. The day was spent with Arm Drill & General Cleaning.

October 5th
We were relieved in LANCASTER LINES by the Royal Fusiliers at midday & marched back to ANNEQUIN, after a short rest here, the whole Brigade

Oct 5 (cont'd)
was formed up and marched
to BETHUNE, where we billeted
for the night.

Oct 6th
We paraded early this morning
and march via CHOQUES to
BUSNES arriving at 12 noon.
A Battalion roll call was taken,
Latrines, grease pits & incinerators
dug. The men then settled down
to a much needed rest.

Oct 7th
The Battalion is resting & training
at the same time, especial
attention being paid to Bombing
dipping & the smart appearance
of the men.
Lt Bell is appointed Bombing
Officer.

Oct 8th
The weather is still beautiful. The
Men have been practising today
in forming up for dipping
by night, with alarms etc.
Company & Battalion drill
including Bombing
instruction for both
Officers & Men.

Oct 9th
　The best part of the day was spent in digging of trench for training of Bombers.
　Physical, Arm, & company Drill was also the order of the day.

Oct 10th
　Nearly all the Battalion had baths today at GUARDBECQUE. There was a Church Parade at Battn Parade Ground at 11:30, & 200 men continuing the work of digging the Bombing trench.

Oct 11th
　There was no early parade this morning. The Battalion paraded for a route march, the route taken being BUSNES – LA MIQUELERIE – LA PIERRIERE – EPINATE – BILLETS. In the afternoon three companys practiced at the Rifle Range at HOLLANDERIE.

Oct 12th
　The Battalion this morning received instruction in Bombing up a New French Platoon Bombing parties practiced with dummy rounds & connecting

Oct 12th (Contd)

captured trenches. Also he
arranged for supplying Bombs
and attacking trenches etc.
Lt's Frisby & Brabazon went out
for instruction by Divisional Staff
on Tactical Scheme.
2 Lt. Mills proceeded to WISQUE
on a one days course of the
LEWIS gun.

Oct 13th

150 men practised on the
HOLLANDERIE Rifle Range.
The remainder went by Companies
to the Bombing trench where
schemes drafted by the
Company Commanders were
practised.
General Weir took over command
of the 74th Inf. Brigade in place
of Gen. Finch-Peace who went
to England.
Divisional General Bripps took
over command of 25th Division
in place of Maj. Gen. Bulfin
who went to England.
The new programme of work
for bios drill etc after
2.0 pm.

October 14th
All the men who did not have
Baths at the beginning of the
week bathed today.
The men having been refitted
a through inspection was held
this morning.
The Officers paraded under Lt BELL
who gave them instruction
in Bomb throwing.
In the afternoon we played
the 1st Welsh at Rugger, a
most exciting game resulted
in victory for us by 19 points
to 3 points.

October 15th
The day was commenced by Physical
Drill, which is now throughly
enjoyed by all ranks.
The C.O inspected the Billets.
kit, & Transport.
Bombing squads were under
instruction with live bombs.
Lt MILLS commenced a new
class of instruction on the
LEWIS GUN, every man and
Officer in future has to have
a thorough knowledge of
this Gun.

Oct 16th
Weather fine, & usual programme is being carried out.
Major C.L. Graham of the 4th Hussars, & late Commandant of an Entrenching Battalion arrived to take over command.

Oct 17th
To-day being Sunday, Church Parades were held in the morning. In the afternoon we played the 1st Welsh at Rugger and a keenly contested game resulted in a draw.

Oct 18th
We paraded early & marched off via the Canal to HINGES, where we waited over two hours for the 3rd East Surreys to vacate their Billets, which later on we took over, nothing else was done during the day.

Oct 19th
Major C.L. Graham had orders to leave us & join the Royal Fusiliers. Captain C.B.S. Carleton again took over command.
We vacated our Billets at HINGES & marched to ESSARS, where we settled down.

Oct 20th

Rumours are flying around, our maps have been recalled, & no definite programme of work has been arranged.

In the afternoon an inter battalion match was played A & B v. C & D, this resulted in a victory for C & D.

Oct 21st

Other Regiments have orders to clear up & be prepared for a sixty hour train journey, some big move is on, in which we are apparently a necessity.

Oct 22nd

The whole Division is moving, we are being left behind because no Territorials attached to a Brigade can be moved out of the country by either Brigade or Division. We are temporaly posted to the 1st Corps for instructions & assistance. Bombs & all surplus stores have been dumped on us. They have also taken our Field Kitchens. We receive definite orders to move tomorrow.

6th Battn. Welch Regiment.

23rd October – 31st October 1915

October 23rd
We are attached to the 3rd Brigade 1st Divisionen & after a very excellent march in every way reported ourselves to the 3rd Brigade at BURBURE, a good sized mining village, in which all the men are billeted.

Oct 24th
A programme of work was carried out this morning consisting of Platoon & Arm Drill, also practice with smoke Helmets. In the afternoon we played the 2nd Welch at Rugby & beat them by one try to nothing.

Oct 25th
Church Parades were held today, other than that, the day was one of complete rest.

Oct 26th
A programme of work consisting of Physical drill, attacking & Bombing etc was carried out during the morning.
In the afternoon a Brigade Boxing contest was held at which some very spectacular bouts were witnessed

Oct 27th

The men practised the Attack, & advancing in Artillery formation working in conjunction with the Bombers, during the morning.
In the afternoon the finals for the boxing competition were held, none of our men got past the semi-finals

Oct 28th

One Company consisting of 200 men marched off to join other Companies of the Brigade & were inspected by H.M. the King. The unfavourable weather rather marred the proceedings.
The usual morning's programme was also suspended owing to the rain.

Oct 29th.

Owing to the heavy rain, the morning's programme was postponed, and in its place, Billets were thoroughly cleaned, and inspected the personel was also totaled up.

Oct 30th

Between showers the first morning's parade consisting of Company Close order drill was held, later the C.O. inspected Kits.

In the afternoon we were to have played the 2nd Welsh, but owing to the inclement weather, it was postponed until the following Saturday.

Oct 31st

Weather still cold & wet. Church Parade on Battn Parade ground.

Captain F.A.S. HINTON rejoined the Battalion.

www.ingramcontent.com/pod-product-compliance
Lightning Source LLC
Chambersburg PA
CBHW081244170426
43191CB00034B/2039